Don't Dumb Down Your Greatness

Anthony Frasier

www.anthonyfrasier.com

ISBN 978-0-692-67187-0

Printed in the United States of America

Version 1.5

Edited by Shavonta Arline

Use the hashtag **#DDDYG** when discussing the book
on social media!
Join my email list on **AnthonyFrasier.com**

 @AnthonyFrasier

 @AnthonyFrasier

 AntFrasier

 Soundcloud.com/AnthonyFrasier

*DEDICATED TO CYNTHIA & WILLIAM R.
FRASIER. MY MOTHER AND BROTHER. YOUR
SACRIFICES CHANGED MY LIFE. I LOVE YOU.*

CONTENTS

PREFACE: MY STORY - PART ONE

Let's take a quick trip to the past.

When I was a youngster, I struggled with childhood depression. When I was in fifth grade, about 11 years old, I was a short and chubby kid. I lived with my mother and brother in a one-bedroom apartment in Newark, NJ. I grew up in a neighborhood infested with drugs, gangs, and crime. My parents got divorced when I was young, and my mother raised the two of us by herself. Things were not easy for us, but that didn't stop me from keeping a smile ,on my face.

My mother was strict. With the prevalence of neighborhood kids getting sucked into street life, my mother didn't want us to fall into the wrong crowd. The only place in the neighborhood we were allowed to go was to our front porch, backyard, or to our grandparent's home, which was right next door. From my home, I jealously eyed my classmates riding their bikes in the street.

To escape the strict regulation of my mother's rules, I looked forward to school where I could interact with the kids I was never allowed to play with at home. When I was at school, I wanted to be the cool kid. So I drew graffiti art on notebook paper to impress my classmates. I would even do drawings for girls I liked, thinking that would get me closer to them.

For a while, things at school were going well, but they took a turn for the worst for me during that year when I began to get teased and bullied because of my height and weight. During gym class, I would be the last picked to be on a team. I can recall coming back to school after Christmas break and a girl sitting next to me was so disgusted that she went to the teacher and asked if she could switch seats. I was so embarrassed.

During that year, there were times I would pretend to go to school in the morning. I would wait until my mother left for work and then sneak back into the house. That optimistic kid always wearing a smile, was gone. My love for going to school grew into hate.

In addition, my attitude did a complete flip. I didn't care about anything. I got into fights, I knew couldn't win (in hindsight that was hilarious). I began talking back to adults. My grades started slipping. My mother was at the school for parent-teacher conferences so much, they knew her by her first name.

But nothing was worse than the day I earned a nickname that would haunt me for years. My brother used to always joke about Biggie Smalls songs. He came up with fake raps and acted out a fictional character named Piggy Balls. I loved to join in the jokes, and we would make our own versions of Biggie Smalls raps under that persona. Then, I decided to bring the joke to school with me. This was not a good idea.

In an attempt to do something that would lead to acceptance at school, I recorded one of the songs on a cheap recorder. It backfired on me immediately. Sure they laughed, but it wasn't with me, it was at me. From that point on, the kids started to call me Piggy. I don't recall any of the kids even using my real name anymore.

This nickname followed me up until I actually graduated from middle school. It was embarrassing. It reminded me every day that I wasn't normal, accepted, cool, and far from great. What I'm not particularly proud of, is that I accepted it. When someone called me outside of my name I would smirk, but my insides were hurt. At this point, as you can probably imagine, my self-esteem was shot. I wasn't sure I could ever recover from it.

The state of mind that I was less than those around me followed me into high school. It made me a quiet kid, and outcast of some sort. I hung out with a group of kids who kind of felt the same way. All we would do after school is go back to each other's houses and play video games. Excluded from the parties, dating, athletics of our classmates, we did nothing.

During lunch breaks at school, I'd sneak into the computer lab or the library to play on the computer. This is where I began to experiment with coding. Yet despite my new hobby, I was so unmotivated by school, that I was one bad grade away from not graduating. So I forced myself to hit the books and earned enough credits for a diploma. On graduation day one of the teachers from my first year of high school pulled me to the side. He handed me an envelope on my way out.

On the first day of my Freshman year of high school, that same teacher had all the students write a letter to themselves. We weren't allowed to read it until four years later. So I stared at it, almost scared to read what I wrote, but I did...I opened the letter.

The rest is to be continued...

THE INTRO

"See everything fresh and "without form"–then make forms that will express us truthfully and totally and by this certainly free us eventually." – Amiri Baraka, Technology & Ethos

Almost everything I thought I knew about entrepreneurship was a lie.

For the past two years prior to penning these words, I've served, in-person over 2,500 entrepreneurs. I created a platform to learn, engage, and challenge some of the biggest names in the tech industry.

However, during that time, I became acutely aware that people who looked like me were visibly absent from mainstream representations of the tech industry. If you were watching TV or scanning entrepreneurship magazines you'd hardly see a person of color. But we exist.

I've spoken at tech conferences all over the country, and when I hit the stage at each of the conferences that I held, I was always in awe of the turnout. A sea of black faces coming together to learn, build, and network. In my heart, I was happy to be apart of the larger community of tech professionals and entrepreneurs. Yet, if I would've listened to the subtle hints in the media at the time suggesting that the tech field was not for the melanin-rich skin that eagerly gathered together in those settings, then I would have packed up and left before even starting. But I didn't, because, despite the messages that were being sent by the larger media, I had a message of my own to share. I'm here to tell it.

A few years ago, I took some time out to mentor a young man who wanted to be an entrepreneur. I asked him what his biggest challenge was? He said he was scared. I asked for more information to pinpoint his area of fear and what he shared is common to many in his shoes. He didn't know how to network, stay focused, he feared failure, and lacked self-confidence. He also argued that he'd be overlooked by customers because he was black. As I sat and listened, I felt that I was hearing a voice from the other side of my mirror. He reminded me of myself.

There was a time when I felt the same way. I started to give him some tips on what I learned on my journey, and saw how delighted he was. I never had anyone tell me what to look out for, and what not to do. I didn't have exposure to many entrepreneurs who looked like me, especially in tech. So, I wasn't privileged to have conversations like that in my neighborhood, or at my dinner table.

Throughout my career, I've often looked back over my choices and experiences to extract meaning. I've also often wondered how many other young black entrepreneurs were like that young man I spoke to: lost and in need of mentorship seemingly where none existed. When I decided to write this book it was with a goal to package what I felt could positively transform a young person's view of entrepreneurship. So, I wrote it like I was talking to my 16-year-old self. What could I say to prepare him for the challenges he is about to face? How could I help him avoid certain obstacles? What could I tell him that he'd otherwise have to learn the hard way?

My goal is to be a big brother figure to the young people in black communities. We face certain challenges that are unique. We aren't using our gifts, we are just buying gifts. According to research by Neilson, African American buying power was $1 trillion in 2015. Yet, our money is going out of our community at an exponentially faster rate than it is being deposited. It's time to invest in ourselves through consciousness and currency.

In addition to imparting the importance of financially investing in our communities, I have a goal to instill pride in our youth that will serve as a foundational stepping stone to tapping into their potential. Their success depends on it. A study by Ming-Te Wang of the University of Pittsburgh and Harvard University's James P. Huguley reinforces the notion that cultural and racial pride is paramount to individual and collective success in that "When African American parents instill a proud, informed, and sober perspective of race in their sons and daughters, these children are more likely to experience increased academic success."

This is great insight that young people do better in school when they are confident in who they are. However, I would propose to take it a step further and suggest that the same confidence also has an effect in all other areas of your life. Entrepreneurship like school is a series of lessons and tests that come with rewards.

This is why it's, as this book title suggests, it is crucial that we don't dumb down our greatness. With this in mind, I constructed the areas of most importance that I thought readers would benefit from and divided them into chapters that will cover:

How to create luck

Foster creativity

Identify who real friends are in business

Get rid of self-doubt

Deal with haters

Set goals

Create good habits

Become more patient.

And much more.

Like the young man mentioned earlier, people often fear what they don't understand. Yet, the clearer we can make the path, the more people will travel it fearlessly.

In each chapter, I will give advice that I wish someone would have given me when I first started out. When I learned each of these skills I became a better entrepreneur, but most of all a better person. I'm on a quest to be great, and I'm bringing you along with me.

Finally, whether you bought this book or got it free, please share it. If you see it online, steal it. I'm giving you permission. As long as you pass it along to a young person who wants to become an entrepreneur, or just starting out as one, you're helping with my goal to influence 100,000+ young black lives in the next year through every piece of content that I make.

Thanks for reading. Be great, and never stop learning.

HUSTLE + OPPORTUNITY + OPTIMISM = LUCK

"I'm a greater believer in luck, and I find the harder I work the more I have of it" – Thomas Jefferson

When I was 16 years old I met Monte Lipman, the founder of Universal Records (now Republic Records). His personal driver dropped him off in an all black S-Class Mercedez Benz Sedan in front of my high school. I'd never seen anything like it. It was a special career day held on a Saturday and he was the only thing that could get me out of bed before Noon on the weekend.

In case you're not familiar, Monte Lipman was the guy who ran the music industry. Artists like Nelly, Cash Money, Akon and more were under his umbrella. I had dreams of being in the music industry myself, so my goal was to network and get some tips. He gave a speech, and before he left I looked him in his eyes and said, "this won't be the last time we meet".

I don't remember anything from his speech except for his recipe for getting lucky. It's the recipe he says he has followed, and got him to where he is in life. So, a curious kid like myself paid close attention to every word as he detailed the plan that I knew would lead to success. Here's what he wrote on the chalkboard:

Preparation + Opportunity = Luck

It was the first time I had seen the word "luck" used in a way that didn't have a magical undertone. Usually the word "luck" conjures up thoughts of four leaf clovers, blowing out birthday candles or throwing coins in a pond. Never did I imagine luck as something I could create with my own effort. But it made sense.

According to him, by staying prepared, if an opportunity would arise you would get "lucky." I later found out that the quote originated from the old philosopher Seneca who said: *"Luck is what happens when preparation meets opportunity."*

There's something worth taking to heart from the words of Mr. Lipman and Seneca, but I want to change that equation a bit and add a new twist to it. This time, it goes like this:

Hustle + Opportunity + Optimism = Luck

Years after meeting Monte, that quote stayed in my head. I tried to stay prepared as I went about my entrepreneurial pursuits in anticipation of the perfect opportunity presenting itself. Yet, I failed so many times, but in my mind the failure was preparation. Life was preparing me and getting me ready for the right opportunity. Those opportunities came, and they still continue to come. But my discovery was that they only came when I hustled. Preparation is a substitute for hard work and hustle. I'll break down this entire equation the way I see it.

Hustle

Hard work – Knowing something is going to be hard, makes it easier. Setting realistic expectations will better prepare you to exceed them. Many people think getting lucky involves no hard work, but that's a big misconception.

Of course, there are people in the world who do little and get so much. But, either they had to do the hard work, their parents had to, or great grandparents had to. Somebody had to do the hard work at some moment in time. If you're like me, and you don't come from wealth, then your own effort is what matters the most.

Persistence – They say persistence is "genius in disguise", and now I know why. If you want to lose weight you have to eat well and exercise consistently. If you want to be a good artist, you have to draw consistently. If you want to shoot a basketball like Steph Curry, then you should be in the gym shooting consistently. See the pattern here?

Greatness comes from practice. Don't be fooled by the perception of effortlessness. Whatever you aim to do, be consistent and persistent. This will separate you from the crowd. I always think of the 48 Laws Of Power by Robert

Greene, when I approach the topic of persistence and greatness. He says:

"Your actions must seem natural and executed with ease. All the toil and practice that go into them, and also all the clever tricks, must be concealed. When you act, act effortlessly, as if you could do much more. Avoid the temptation of revealing how hard you work—it only raises questions."

Perseverance – No matter how hard you work, and how persistent you are, life gets in the way in the form of obstacles and setbacks. To the untrained eye, these challenges can appear disguised as clues that it's time to quit, but they are not necessarily so. Your response to them is everything, and perseverance is key. Perseverance is what keeps your engine going, long after you run out of gas. It's your crazy factor. It's also known as hunger. How hungry are you for your desired goal? These are the questions you won't know the answer to until the situation faces you head on. In the words of Jay Z *"The genius thing we did was, we didn't give up."*

Opportunity

Hustle creates opportunity – if you hustle hard enough, people will notice you. They will want to associate with you, do deals with you, invest in you, partner with you, buy from you, or hire you. When we began to do events for my last company, The Phat Startup, we did them monthly. Because our events were held at a regular interval, people began to notice our consistency with hosting a monthly gathering. Eventually, these events led to people writing about us and landing even bigger and better guests that would attend. We created the opportunities to grow through consistency.

Vision – Many opportunities will come your way through the efforts of your hustle, but not all of them will. There are times when you can spot an opportunity as well. But having an eye for the right open door takes practice. Without the ability to see opportunities, you can be sitting right in front of one, and pass it by. The reason we often don't see opportunities is because they often look like insurmountable obstacles rather than open doors.

For example, losing a job can seem like a terrible situation to the untrained eye. When you are used to going to a place of business to earn a steady paycheck, the loss of that income stream can be a devastating blow. But, in fact, it may not be what it looks like. Your mind will either process it as a bad thing (misfortune) or a good thing (opportunity). Although it may be true that you no longer have a "job" it's not necessarily true that you don't have any opportunities. Many successful people have found themselves in that exact situation and used it as a launchpad to recognizing their dreams. So if you're in a position where it seems as though every door around you is closing remember what Richard Branson says: *"Business opportunities are like buses, there's always another one coming."*

Optimism

Faith – The Bible defines faith as *"the substance of things hoped for, the evidence of things not seen."* By this definition, faith is an essential element of the desires of our heart. It is part and parcel of having a dream because dreams rely on faith as it is a part of their very "substance" So if you haven't reached your goal yet, it is paramount that you have complete confidence that you will. It will make all the difference in whether you do or not.

Meditation – In the words of James Altucher, *"anxiety and gratitude can't live in the same head."* If you're an entrepreneur or an aspiring one, I probably don't have to tell you about the gut-wrenching effects of anxiety on your body and mind. Left unchecked, anxiety can keep us from productivity as we wrestle with everything that could go wrong and stress about everything that we cannot control. One of the best ways to deal with anxiety is through mediation.

Meditation is the 20 minutes a day you spend focusing on your motivation. It's a way to practice being grateful for everything you already have and clearing your mind off the worry and doubt that can sabotage your goals if you let it run wild. Meditation keeps you grounded among all the craziness of life.

Personal health (only what you have control over) – It's hard to be optimistic when you are sick. Your health plays a part in your attitude, which plays a huge part in your effort, which plays a part in your success. As long as you are trying to get better at least 1% a day, your attitude will feed off your progress.

Luck

When you hustle hard to create opportunities while always expecting to win, you generate luck. It doesn't get any more technical than that. Luck is not about laziness, it's not about sitting on the sidelines and expecting a handout. Luck is a hustler's secret weapon. It's the fruit of his labor. Uncross your fingers, and get to work.

I blogged about this topic not too long before writing this book. In the post, I also mentioned Monte Lipman and how his quote inspired me. Two months after writing that post, he emailed me, saying he loved it. He told me he was now adopting my version of the luck equation in all of his talks moving forward. All I kept thinking about was the last thing I told him 15 years ago, "this won't be the last time we meet." Now, this connection has renewed. I made it happen...with hustle, opportunity, and optimism, I got lucky.

BEING FRIENDS VS. BEING COOL

Real friends, how many of us?
How many of us, how many jealous? Real friends
It's not many of us, we smile at each other
But how many honest? Trust issues – Kanye West

Relationships make the world go around. You've probably heard the saying that when it comes to success "it's not what you know but who you know," and in many ways this is very true. There are are several instances throughout life where you will find that being connected with the right people opens doors and introduces opportunities that you may have not otherwise had access to. Indeed, relationships are important, but of equal importance is recognizing what kind of relationships you need to fulfill the goals you have in life.

In general, relationships can fall into two broad categories: personal and business. Personal relationships include family, friends and romantic interests. In short, personal relationships nurture your heart and emotional well-being.

Business relationships potentially affect your educational, business and career pursuits. These often include classmates, colleagues, associates and others that you may personally "know" but are not personally "close" to. Where personal relationships nurture your heart and emotional well-being, business relationships exist to ultimately foster your pockets.

For the purposes of this chapter, we will look at the difference between the personal relationships you have with "friends" and the professional relationships you have with those you are "cool" with. As you matriculate through life and business it will serve you well to recognize the difference between the two.

In Merriam-Webster's dictionary, the definition of a friend is *"one attached to another by affection or esteem."* We start making friends with people very early in life as children. When we are very young friendships are pure and unmotivated by self-gain. There are no worries about backstabbers, manipulation, fake love, or snake behavior. Friendships are genuine and sincere. They are also simple and centered on having fun: playing video games, tag, and sleep-overs.

As we get older, friendships become more complicated. We grow apart from the people we were friends with as kids. Lives grow in different directions and our circle gets smaller. Because of this, if we are mature, we become way more invested in the relationships we have with our friends. Friends are people we rely on and trust in, they are are people who go to bat for us and may even put their lives on the line for us. Friends are there for us when we are down and out. Friends do so much for us, and real ones are rare.

When you first started your business, chances are you told a friend you trust about it. They may not have fully understood what you were about to get into but, like a real friend, they were excited for you. They sat and let you pour out every fear, worry, idea, high and low because they love you.

As you begin to go out into the business world you will attend events, meetups, conferences, and expos. You will shake many hands and start to talk to people outside of your small circle of friends who know more about your entrepreneurial interests than your friends may. This may excite you. It may make you feel drawn to them. This is great, it's what you should be doing. These relationships have the potential to open wide the floodgates of opportunities and success if you are smart about them, and by smart I mean if you are able to recognize these relationships and people for what they are. Essentially, these are not people you are going to be friends with, but they are absolutely people you should be cool with.

Be Cool

Wilson Mizner once said, *"Be nice to people on your way up because you'll meet them on your way down."*

That's a great way to broadly encompass what it means to

be cool. In my own words, being cool is being a person of value. Being resourceful and able to hook people up, make connections, give advice, and help bring increase to many lives. Yet, unlike being a friend, being cool involves expecting nothing in return. You do it because you care about being an asset, not because you're interested in reciprocation.

Now, you may be getting confused because some aspects of being cool sound a lot like being friends with people. It's true that some of the actions of cool people mimic the actions of friends, yet there is one key line of division: friends put their hearts on the line by being vulnerable and expecting each other to value, nurture and love to the same standard. Being cool, however, involves protecting yourself from potentially devastating disappointment by having no personal expectations of your business relationships. You will notice opportunities open up to you more when you embody this philosophy.

Let's go back to our friend Merriam-Webster and explore a derivative of the word "friend" and find out the essence of being friendly. In that same dictionary, you can find this definition of friendly: *"showing kindly interest and goodwill."* If you'll recall, the definition of friend concerned itself with emotions and affection, in other words, feelings, while being friendly is concerned with "doing". Friend and friendly are clearly different. You don't need to be a deep friend to help transform someone's life or show goodwill, and in fact, getting too deep can be harmful to you as an entrepreneur.

Problems will begin when you try to become "friends"

with some of the people you meet and do business with that you were meant to be "cool" with.

The reason this can become problematic is because when you give people you hardly know a label that stands for much more (such as a friend), you start to hold them to standards they never agreed upon, or may not even be interested in. Thus, setting yourself up to get hurt.

This does not mean you become an asshole or don't help people, it also doesn't mean that just because someone isn't a "friend" that they can't provide an immensely positive relationship. This book is not encouraging you to be a jerk to people because you're not friends with them, in fact, it's teaching the exact opposite. This is about protecting yourself and making wise decisions free of unnecessary emotions. I'll give you an example.

A buddy of mine became "friends" with a group of connected young investors. He'd go to events with them, go out for drinks, have deep conversations, etc. The connection he created was so great, you'd think he was part of the crew. Then one day the invites stopped. He felt they were being phony and his feelings were hurt.

Shortly after he asked me for some business suggestions on how to handle a new challenging situation. I advised my buddy to reach out to that same group for a collaboration. I figured they would be able to help him. He declined because he felt they treated him like chopped liver. He was so blinded by his anger, it impacted his decision making. He let his feelings get the best of him. He took a non-invite to hang out personal, and it hurt his business.

You see, according to the group he had been hanging out with, everything was just fine. Their perception of him hadn't been changed or negatively impacted until they recognized his reaction when the invitations to hang out slowed down.

Ever heard the term "business is never personal"? You'll experience that many times as an entrepreneur. It's hard to not take things personal when your livelihood, future, and money is on the line. But you have to practice being stoic. Or like I like to say…be cool

Being cool means you validate yourself. You don't need anyone to cosign you or whatever you are working on. You know that you are great. Never stress about getting accolades, and recognition that you see so many others receive. If you seek others to validate you, you will become a hater over time.

Being cool is freedom. It's your way of detaching yourself from drama or overreaction. If my buddy had known that, he wouldn't have blown a landmark deal for himself. Trying to be friends with everyone you meet is self-sabotage. Being cool with everyone you meet creates abundance and clarity of mind that you are making decisions based on what is truly best for you, not only on what feels good to you. .

Being cool means you are confident with your goals. It means no one can take you away from your destiny. If someone didn't return the favor you did for them, don't take it personally. When you don't get that speaking gig you've been emailing for even though you vouched for someone involved in the planning of the event, don't take it personally. When you don't get that investment in your company from a VC, don't take it personally. That opportunity will return, or a better one will take place.

Finally, remember to be genuine. Smart people can sense foul motives, that will turn them off from working with you and likewise, if someone doesn't have the right energy, separate yourself from them. Don't compromise who you are for a check. Don't try to manipulate someone to get an upper hand. It won't turn out good in the end. The only way to be sure you won't lose anything is by being yourself. What's meant for you, is meant for you.

When expecting an immediate return from someone you are cool with, you'll end up upset when you don't get it. On the flip side, when you're not expecting an immediate return from someone, the payback will come when you least expect it. In fact, it may even be better than you could have ever imagined. Don't look for people to pay you back, look for life to pay you back.

It's also important for me to note that this doesn't mean you won't make true friends on your entrepreneur journey. You will. I have made friends in this business, but you better believe we were just cool at first.

JUST ADD WATER

"The wealthiest places in the world are not gold mines, oil fields, diamond mines or banks. The wealthiest place is the cemetery. There lies companies that were never started, masterpieces that were never painted... In the cemetery, there is buried the greatest treasure of untapped potential. There is a treasure within you that must come out. Don't go to the grave with your treasure still within you." – Myles Munroe

This in the 90's black classic comedy film *Friday*, main character Craig (played by Ice Cube) goes into the kitchen to make a bowl of cereal but discovers he doesn't have any milk. His father comes into the kitchen and spots him attempting to throw the cereal away. He immediately yells at him and says *"You better put some water on that damn shit."*

Some of you may have similar memories, and what Craig tried to do when he saw that he didn't have all the things he needed for a bowl of cereal is a metaphor for what so many entrepreneurs do. When they get an idea, the moment they don't have all the necessary ingredients, they throw it away. Aspiring entrepreneurs love to push the goal line, finding any excuse on why it couldn't get done. My response? *"You better put some water on that damn shit."*

I can remember being hungry on days we had no groceries in the house when I was a child. I would go into the kitchen, look around in the cabinets, and it would be small portions of food or nothing at all. So I would think of ways to combine the ingredients to make a larger meal. My mother taught me not to waste food, so I used whatever I had.

If you've ever been in a place where you didn't have everything you needed to see a dream come true, you are not alone. I've had the same challenges before. Maybe you have an idea for an app but you don't know how to code, so your idea seems out of reach. Or perhaps you don't have any money, so you can't get that project off the ground. You don't have any connections, so you feel that you can't be featured in a certain magazine. These are the challenges that can often stop an entrepreneur right in their tracks.

If this sounds like you, open your mind to the possible resources you do have available to replace the ones you don't. If the door is shut, find a window. If there is no milk, add that damn water. By doing this, you foster the most underrated skill in business today: Creativity. Creativity lives in that gap between what you want, and what you don't have. Forcing you to find ways to make things happen without the resources you need.

Sheena Allen is the perfect example of someone who used what she had. Sheena is a successful tech entrepreneur from Terry, Mississippi. She has an app company with millions of downloads and celebrity endorsements. She has no coding background, is a black woman, and lives thousands of miles from Silicon Valley.

She got the idea for her first app after a trip to Wal-Mart with her college roommate. Frustrated with the task of keeping up with her finances, she longed for an app to help. When she couldn't find one, she decided to make it herself. She booted up Microsoft Word and designed her first app. She didn't read articles on the best software to design apps, she used a typical word processor. Using squares, odd shapes, and clip art to describe the different screens.

Once she was ready to get it developed, all she did was Google "find iPhone developer." She landed on a website called Guru and linked up with a developer from Canada. She used her savings to get the first app built within a month. When I asked Sheena what was the thinking behind her moves? She replied, "I had no idea what I was doing."

Today, her company *Sheena Allen Apps* enjoys a whole variety of mobile apps. All her lack of resources and skills became assets. Sure, she made some mistakes along the way, but they became learning experiences in the end. She got creative, got bold, and was passionate about solving her problem.

Compare her to the "could have been" entrepreneurs that often gives up on their dreams when they see the roadblocks that face them. These are the people who are still sleeping on themselves and their dreams. They are still telling stories of what they need to get started instead of taking a leap and trusting in their own creativity. If Sheena had the access most Silicon Valley entrepreneurs have, would she be as successful? The creativity you develop will often give you a better result than if you had all the money in the world.

Another great thing about creativity is, it has the potential to attract what you need. When people see that you can get things done without them, that's when they begin to come to you. My brother used to give me a talk every day about women. He'd say things like *"just get your money up and focus on you, everything else will fall into place."* The message in his words was that I should be chasing my dreams and having the time of my life and at the right time, the right woman would notice and invite herself into the situation.

I can't promise you will find the love of your life by working hard, but the advice works for entrepreneurship. Investors want to put their money behind the guy who found a way despite the odds. Corporations want to work with the girl that got 1 million users, with no advertising budget. You can't get a record deal unless you have shown that you can create your own audience and buzz first.

How to be creative

There are no standard rules to follow when creatively getting things done. Every situation is different, but here are a few things I do myself that can give you a starting point.

#1 Leverage Your Network: Sometimes you already know the connection that you are looking to network with. Put any ego you have to the side, and contact people you already have a relationship with. Dig deep. Also, it's good to let people know what you are working on publicly to some degree. When they know what you have going on and are willing to assist, they may just come to you.

#2 Start Small: When I created my meetup group in Newark, I partnered with local organizations in my hometown. My goal was to get the big partners, but they wouldn't even take a phone call if I tried. Being consistent and building a solid reputation among smaller partners, earned me larger ones. Also, smaller partners can lead to better opportunities.

#3 Research Alternatives: Google it. Can't get access to something or someone? Google alternatives, or people doing the same work. This research may lead you to finding just what you were looking for your to accomplish your goal.

#4 Do it yourself: I wanted to get an internship at a startup but didn't know how to code. So, I went to the library every morning like it was my job. I didn't become Mark Zuckerberg, but I learned enough to land a life-changing opportunity. If you have the time and patience, learning new skills is a worthwhile investment.

#5 Read Books or Look at Interviews: I learned a while ago that success leaves clues. I read books from people who

have already faced the challenges I'm currently facing. These days you can even get tons of advice right on YouTube. Take advantage.

Those are just a few ways you can begin to foster some creative thinking on your challenges. So Identify the one thing stopping you right now from chasing your dreams. Get creative, and find a way to make it happen no matter what. Don't give up, you better add that water!

THE HATER IN YOUR HEAD

"They don't want you to win" – DJ Khaled

In 2015, well-known Hip Hop figure DJ Khaled rose to popularity on the platform Snapchat. Snapchat allows you to create time-sensitive video clips in chronological order called, "stories." Khaled's videos are fueled by motivational messages and keys to success.

Some of these keys are jokes, but Khaled's keeping it real most of the time. He's aware he has become a meme and cashed in on it with his 6 million viewers.

Khaled has an archenemy, he refers to as *"THEY."* So throughout the day he says things like:

"THEY don't want you to win."

"THEY don't want you to eat."

"THEY don't want you to have success."

"Watch out for *THEY!"*

THEY have become the world's biggest group of haters. In order for you to become successful in life, you have to know how to handle THEY.

Even though DJ Khaled speaks of a *THEY* that exists in the world around him, I feel like *THEY* can be in our own head sometimes. That's right, we can be our own hater.

I once spoke to a friend about his writing skills. He had given me a preview of his new book and even though I loved it, he decided to scrap it. So I asked him why he chose to do this. His reason was that nobody would like it. He doubted his abilities to write a good book, feared criticism, and as a result killed off his dream. He was a perfectionist, always trying to make the perfect product, and when he felt that he didn't measure up, he chopped himself down.

He is not alone. People often create this false group of haters in their head, envisioning bad outcomes. We call this self-doubt. Doubting yourself is dream cancer. Especially since the biggest secret in the world is: Nobody knows what they are doing! But most of us think that there is always someone out there who has it "more" together than we do, so we count ourselves out before anyone else has a chance to.

I happened to be watching DJ Khaled videos and told my friend to look along with me. He wasn't ready to deal with the haters in the real world if he hadn't dealt with the ones in his head yet. We should aspire to be like DJ Khaled, and declare war on the *THEY* in our minds.

Have you ever noticed in Hip Hop culture, haters are

always a topic of discussion? These haters rarely exist. They are a figment of the imagination existing only in the rapper's mind for the purpose of giving them motivation, and something to fight against.

In the book "*33 Strategies of War*" by Robert Greene, the first strategy is self-directed war. His theory is that you cannot win any fight if you can't control your thinking. His advice? To wage ruthless and continual battle on the enemies within you.

There is nothing wrong with being your biggest critic. But, there is everything wrong with being your biggest hater.

Here are some ways to quiet the voices of doubt in your head:

#1 Realize that you are not an impostor. You really are as good as you think you are. When an entrepreneur reaches some level of success sometimes it's hard for them to believe it. Even if it's a small level of wins. I suffered from childhood depression, so I wasn't used to good things happening to me when I got older. It kind of made me uncomfortable. I would get interviews from major magazines, awards, TV commercials, and documentary features. I couldn't believe that anyone would want to recognize my work so I would think to myself questions like "do I deserve all this?"

It's called Impostor Syndrome. This is an actual condition discovered by clinical psychologists in the 80's. It's used to describe individuals who aren't able to accept their accomplishments. These individuals are always in fear they will get exposed at any moment for being a fraud. Sound familiar? Practice doing small celebrations when you do something. Accept your wins!

#2 Don't compare yourself. Everybody has the same color blood. Stop thinking you aren't as smart as someone else you see being successful. The key is to take away the glitter. I learned much of this reading *"The Obstacle Is the Way"* by Ryan Holiday. I discovered Stoics taught their followers to imagine great thinkers having sex. I kid you not. The goal was to get you to see them in their most vulnerable state. Helping you to view them as just human, just like you.

Marcus Aurelius taught his students to take the swag away from people or expensive items in your mind. So fried chicken is simply a dead animal. Soda was just water with flavored syrup. See things and people as they are.

#3 Develop the art of not giving a damn. Some of us spend a lot of time stressing over things and circumstances that we have very little power over. For example, the opinions of others that we have no control over. The only thing you have control over is how much effort you will put into what you want to create. Do your best to deliver the best value in your hustle. After releasing to the public, take the constructive feedback and improve your product, and don't sweat the small stuff.

#4 Set Small Goals. Small goals are smart goals. Many experts are now advising people to focus on the process goals (see chapter "Process Makes Perfect") over large

goals. Small goals help you to develop confidence early. Basketball coaches teach players to shoot near the hoop, to build up confidence before they take a long shot. Embody that same philosophy with goals, and you'll be happier.

#5 Keep a Positive Circle. Positive attracts positive. Who you hang around has everything to do with your thinking. If you stay around negative people you'll become a negative person. Your circle influences your inner thoughts. Not just your friends, but even your family. If you live in a toxic environment, consume as many positive experiences as possible. Also, don't gossip. Gossip only feeds negative thoughts, or worse, it plants them in your head unnecessarily.

#6 Find time to relax and quiet the mind. As entrepreneurs we often spend a lot of time thinking which can be overwhelming and stressful. To remedy this, it is extremely beneficial to get some mental rest and calmness. Deepak Chopra's *"The Seven Spiritual Laws of Success"* quotes Franz Kafka, an Austrian philosopher. *"You need not leave your room. Remain sitting at your table and listen. You need not even listen, simply wait. You need not even wait, just learn to become quiet, and still, and solitary. The world will freely offer itself to you to be unmasked. It has no choice; it will roll in ecstasy at your feet."* Ensuring you get this time of mental calm will help you to put in perspective any illegitimate feelings of self-doubt.

#7 Intend to win. In many ways, winning is a mental conquest. What I mean is that you have to first believe you can be successful if you plan to actually be successful. To accomplish this, set an intention to overcome your fear

of criticism, failure, and lack of experience. When you're intentional, you become self-aware and more prepared to spot those moments of self-sabotage.

#8 Do your homework. People fear what they don't understand. Do as much research as possible on your challenge and watch those voices quiet away as you gain confidence in your knowledge of what to expect and what you are capable of. However, caution yourself to do just enough research to empower you, but not so much to stop you from making a move. In the end, you will likely find that the more knowledgeable you are about your goals, the longer you will stick with them even if you hit a bump in the road along the way.

Learn from this and let it help you become a dope entrepreneur because that's the last thing *THEY* want you to be.

PROCESS MAKES PERFECT

"There's no destination. The journey is all that there is, and it can be very, very joyful" – Srikumar Rao

Goals used to frustrate me. The idea of having goals wasn't the problem but rather the idea of what would be involved in accomplishing them. It stressed me out because nothing is worse than starting a fresh year with so much optimism, to just run out of gas halfway through. Year after year, I experimented with different systems to figure this goal thing out. But then I finally discovered what I was doing wrong. I kept confusing my mission and vision with my goals. Focusing only on your vision which is long term will leave you stressed out in the short term.

Not long ago I read *"The 12 Week Year"* by Brian Moran, and took advice from mentors on developing shorter goals. It just made so much sense to me. Focusing on the next twelve months was just too stressful, but shifting my attention to what I could accomplish in twelve weeks was a pivotal change. This action helped me to develop a laser-like trajectory for achievable goals. The best part is that I never lost sight of my overall vision and mission for goals.

I want to break down how to use 3-month goals in a simple way. It's not about achieving what you might be able to do in a year in three short months. Instead, it's about getting things done a little at a time so that every day you get closer to where you want to be in a year. As simple breakdown is below:

Outcome Goals

Outcome goals define what we want to accomplish at the end of three months. They are realistic and specific. They are also compatible with a three month execution time frame. For example, you may have a goal to write twelve high-quality blog posts in three months. Writing twelve blogs in three months is a realistic goal. Furthermore, if I accomplish it and reset the goal every three months, I would have 48 high-quality blog posts by the end of the year.

We can apply the same line of reasoning to weight loss. For example, I may want to lose twenty pounds in three months. This is also a realistic goal, and if I were to accomplish it and reset the goal, I would have potentially lost 80 pounds by the end of the calendar year.

Of course, all of these goals will require hard work and persistence, but they are not impossible achievements. My suggestion is to have three outcome goals spread out across business and personal.

Performance Goals

For every outcome goal set, there also needs to be a performance goal. Performance goals are important because they outline in specific detail how we are improving weekly. Performance goals are intended to measure progress over a two-week period.

Let's go back to our blog post goal example. Here is what a performance goal would look like for that outcome goal: *In the next two weeks, I will write one blog every Tuesday.*

Sounds simple enough right? You can see we are reverse engineering.

Here's another one: *I will improve my traffic from 500 visits to 1,000 visits by October 30th. (2 weeks from now)*

This goal will make sure my actions are purely working on traffic increasing activities. Maybe I'll pay for ads or maybe I'll get some people to help tweet it. The point is I am working to improve my performance and I have a specific measurement by which I will be assessing it.

Going back to the weight loss goal, we can apply the same method. For example, a performance goal might be: *In the next two weeks, I'm going to walk five miles at least once.*

Two weeks later I may increase the goal and by the third set of two weeks, I'll walk ten miles at least once.

In the performance goal example, there is no question about what activity is going down. The goal is to improve as much as we can week by week. So if I'm blogging once a week, I'll have four blogs in the month. If I'm increasing traffic by 500 visits every two weeks, traffic will go up by 1,000 visits monthly.

Process Goals

Process goals are the last piece of the puzzle. Process goals are the small actions you need to take to get the performance done. Sometimes you won't need process goals if the performance goals cover a simple task. But, sometimes you need to state what needs to happen, in order for this thing to get done.

Todd Herman actually has a formula the created for this in stating: *"Who is going to do What, When, and Where? This will equal Clarity and Momentum"*

For every performance goal ask yourself what is going to be done? When is it going to get done? Where is it going to be done? This makes the path clear for you, potential employees, and partners. You need a clear process if you're easily side-tracked. So let's use my weight loss example and put a process to it: *Walk five miles Friday morning at 5:00 AM down Grove St.*

Compare that with the performance and you can see how clear it makes it.

Performance Goal	Process Goal
In the next 2 weeks, I'm going to walk five miles once.	*Walk five miles Friday morning at 5:00 AM down Grove St.*

Now it's easy for you to put this on your calendar as a task. If it's a business goal, it's easier to list now in your task management tool.

To summarize, long-term goals are easier to manage when they are broken down into three-month increments and categorized into outcome goals, performance goals and process goals. The outcome goal highlights the overall accomplishment we aim to make, the performance goal outlines the manner in which we will measure progress and the process goal highlights the way we will go about accomplishing our goal. Remember that ultimately, commitment to your goals will determine whether or not you reach them. You have to work through the pain and keep focused.

WRITE EVERYTHING DOWN

"If I waited till I felt like writing, I'd never write at all" – *Anne Tyler*

In the modern world, people ditch writing by hand for their phone or computer. Writing by hand is truly a lost art form in the era of technology ripe with apps and gadgets that will do it for us, or at least, simplify the process. I was the biggest *Evernote* user in my crew for a long time, using it for everything from small lists to big ideas. But something happened to me along the way, I started forgetting things. I noticed every time I wrote something on my phone or tablet, I wouldn't even come back to it, so the value of the resource itself diminished.

Eventually, I bought a small notebook to carry with me everywhere I went. In this book, I write ideas, goals, plans for the day, quotes, etc. Over time, the act of manually writing things down aided in remembering them and I became a better entrepreneur because of it.

Writing things on paper has been immensely helpful to

me as an entrepreneur and here are a few other ways it may benefit you:

Ideas on napkins

Your ideas are worth a lot but it's important to get them on paper, whether a notebook, sticky pad or a plain old napkin. We've all heard of tales of entrepreneurs sketching out a business idea on a napkin, and having it turn into the new Google. It can still happen. I'm a huge fan of author James Altucher who encourages people to write down ideas every day. This practice helps to exercise your brain and make you a better and more creative thinker (see chapter Wake Up Rich).

Great ideas come at a moment's notice. You could be sitting at a bus stop, in church, in a meeting, on the phone, and that idea will hit you like lightning. Write it down. Draw it out. What will it look like? How will it work? The best advice someone gave me when writing down ideas? Go back to them a week later, and next to it write the next step you need to make that idea real. I suggest you do it too, but make it realistic.

You learn better

Princeton University's Pam A. Mueller says *"The present research suggests that even when laptops are used solely to take notes, they may still be impairing learning because their use results in shallower processing. In three studies, we found that students who took notes on laptops performed worse on concep-*

tual questions than students who took notes longhand." By this logic, when you read a book, watch lectures online or in school, or take advice from a mentor you should write it down. Over my life, I've remembered the majority of the notes and ideas I've manually written down, but I would be hard pressed to tell you one thing I copied and pasted into Evernote or Google Docs.

Develop a commonplace book

This sort of piggybacks off the last point. Do you have a reference book for your life? That's what a commonplace book can serve as. Commonplace books were used by scholars in the past. Although people rarely use that term anymore, having an intellectual scrapbook is still significant. Inspiration can come to you from any source, so it's good to have all those sources in one place.

If you want to create your own book it's simple. Buy a journal style notebook with a cover made of leather or any tough material. I suggest you go for the blank pages, so you can draw in them. Standard notebooks risk getting torn or easily damaged. This book should be filled with important information, you want to make sure you can easily access for years to come. Things to put in your book include:

- Notes from the books you read
- Notes from interviews you watch
- Sketches for new ideas
- Lists

- Daily reflections
- Quotes and explanations

Helps you achieve your goals

This is perhaps the most important reason to start writing things down on paper. One of the challenges I've had with accomplishing goals in the past was that they were never written down in a place where I could reach them. I had goals written on my phone, but it ultimately wasn't a good tool for me to store my ideas and notes because it was too distracting. With all of the noise from alerts and notifications, I couldn't really reflect on the ideas I had stored inside of it.

Ultimately, writing things down is an act of intention. It gives your ideas increased value in that you actually took the time to write them down. When you jot a note or idea, you are taking yourself seriously enough to go into action for what could be a profitable endeavor. So grab a notebook, find a pen, and get to writing.

YOU CAN'T MICROWAVE SUCCESS

"Patience is bitter, but its fruit is sweet." – Aristotle

I love looking at inspirational quotes on Instagram. I follow accounts that help me dream and inspire me. I love the pages that show off the interiors of the freshest condos and mansions. I follow millionaires and see them go on countless vacations, every season of the year. I follow them because deep down inside I want these same things.

While I aspire to have these things, I'm exposed to the reality of hard work it takes to get them. That's not the case for everyone. Social Media is exposing so many people to the material side of success. We follow rappers, actors, models, and want that life instantly.

We see success stories online and think that it's easy to become an entrepreneur. The people you see online are only showing the glamorous side of life. They don't show the 100 hours of work, just the 40 hours of play. But it's not just social media that makes millennials impatient, it's traditional media too.

Deep down, many of us want to become unicorns. "Unicorns" is a buzz word used in the business world to showcase a wildly unusual success story. For example, the kid who gets one million users of his app overnight is a unicorn. The Flappy Bird creator who earned fifty thousand dollars a day off a mobile game is a unicorn. If you see these unicorns in the media so much, it's natural for you to feel you can have the same level of success. And you can, but there's a slim chance that it will share the same timing.

This is often hard to accept in light of the fact that we are used to getting everything fast these days. Netflix lets me watch a movie when I want. Amazon now offers same day delivery. We love instant gratification so much. Studies show most people click away from a video if it takes more than 10 seconds to load. We're spoiled by the idea of getting everything we want on a microwave timeline.

So what happens when we decide to be an entrepreneur and don't get the cool benefits right away? We quit. We complain. We're confused. We subconsciously want to put success in a microwave and get it on demand. You have to learn how to be patient because what usually looks like an "overnight" success actually took years to accomplish.

Henry Ford said, *"It has been my observation that most people get ahead during the time that others waste."*

During the slow times, the periods where it seems like nothing is really happening is often the best time to focus and plow on toward your goals. If everyone is playing the short game for instant gratification, you win by holding out. Think of it as an investment in yourself. Long as you are working towards getting better every day, that's compound interest.

The smartest investors in the world like Warren Buffet got their fortune by doing this. Buying when everyone else is selling. Not letting the news, media, and influencers dictate their moves. But standing their ground and making decisions from their own research and knowledge. Embody this.

A study by Ayelet Fishbach, a behavioral science professor, believes *"There are big rewards for those who can delay gratification. These people are doing better at school, get better jobs, have more rewarding and stable social relationships and so on. Basically, the research teaches that patience and self-control predict success in life..."* If you don't believe this, take a minute to research some of your favorite entrepreneurs and really read about their story and how long it took them to become a "success." You may be surprised at what you find.

How to be patient

I can't tell you that waiting is easy or fun, but what I can tell you is that it's a reality of the hustle. So here are a few tips to help keep the wait in perspective:

#1 Love What You Do: If you're going to stay on for the long game, you have to have passion. Steve Jobs famously said, *"any rational person would give up."* So he's saying you have to be crazy about it. Being an entrepreneur will make you

feel that you aren't in your right mind at times. During times when I was involved with a project that I wasn't really passionate about, I either did a horrible job, or I quit. Passion will keep you patient.

#2 Think Bigger Than Money: Looking at nice cars, houses and women are great for daydreams, but in reality, success is more than material and status gains. Think about the legacy you want to leave behind, and that will fuel you to hold on longer. If you base your happiness on material things, beware. The moment you lose them, you will also lose the motivation to keep going. Well known entrepreneur Gary Vaynerchuk's goal is to be the owner of the NFL Jets team. That's so big and iconic, money is just the byproduct of that.

#3 Embrace Pain: You will struggle. Things will get rough. Change your perception of those moments to help motivate you. I once heard the story of why golf balls have dimples. The dimples help create lift and allow the balls to travel 3 times farther than a smooth ball would. The dimples represent our struggle. If we don't have them, we wouldn't have the strength go anywhere.

#4 Learn What To Ignore: You know what triggers negative emotions for you better than anyone else. So when you are encountering experiences that spark feelings of jealousy, impatience, and anxiety, make a conscious effort to block them out. This action alone will give you the power to stay in the game.

#5 Build Great Habits: When you get into the rhythm of doing something, it can become second nature. In this case, get in the rhythm of doing small activities that lead

toward your success. You'll be more patient seeing yourself get closer each day, even if only by 1%. New York Times bestselling author Chris Guillebeau revealed to me that he wrote 1000 words a day. He wasn't a "real" writer, so to put out a successful book, this was the habit that brung him closer. Find yours.

Waiting sucks, and nothing I say can really make it suck less. You may be thinking about your bills, kids, responsibilities, and more. But, to get to the good part you have to hold the line if you truly want to accomplish your goals. Stay the course, and have patience. No matter how hard we try, we can't microwave success. Besides, the food that takes longer to cook usually tastes the best.

LEAVE A LASTING IMPRESSION

"Try not to become a man of success, but rather try to become a man of value." – Albert Einstein

The most common business advice you will hear is to "start networking." Traditional advice would be to put on a suit, get some business cards, and start shaking hands. That works for most people, but that hardly worked for me. My idea of networking is "giving value." Giving value is the best way to make sure every interaction you have with someone will get a return. No matter the situation.

What exactly is value? Value is anything that brings a positive transformation to someone's life, big or small.

In the past I've had a hard time networking. I'm what most people call an ambivert. I'm comfortable in social settings, but more comfortable when I'm alone, being creative. So I had to find a way to start attracting individuals using my creativity, rather than my business card. Giving value allows you to use creativity and become magnetic.

When you're magnetic you don't have to chase people or opportunities, they chase you.

Being magnetic means you are a giver. The most successful entrepreneurs I know are the people who give constantly. Givers are confident in their hustle and don't mind helping someone else become successful. Givers receive, they don't take.

Takers are insecure. Takers believe they can't help someone else because that would give that person an edge on them. Takers pretend to be givers until they get what they want. Takers don't understand that there is enough for everyone to eat. One man's success doesn't limit others. Don't be a taker.

I accomplished one of my personal goals this year. This particular goal was to leave a lasting impression on every person I came across. I wanted to inspire, bring increase, and value to as many lives as possible. In short, be a giver.

I went to a networking event, filled with people I met at various moments throughout the year. There were also people who knew of my work just from the internet. I was almost surprised when these people told me about something I created or said that helped them. It felt good to hear that. Especially since my intention was always to leave a lasting impression.

Many people focus on making a good first impression and ignore what it means to make a lasting impression. There is a difference between a first impression and lasting impression. A *first impression* is what someone thinks the moment they interact with you. A *lasting impression* is what someone thinks long after they interact with you. A first impression can be a lasting one, but not in all cases. Here are a few ways to make a great one:

Give a Damn

In order to make a positive lasting impression, you have to care about the well-being of people. When you care, people can tell. When in conversation pay attention, make eye contact and don't look away. When giving a presentation, give it everything you got. When teaching, go over every detail as possible. People will remember you went the extra mile to help them. This is whether they met you in person or even just watched a video of you.

I used to study a small group of internet marketers. I was always amazed at how these guys were making so much money with little details about who they were. They would put up popular logos to establish credibility, but no real background information. Yet, they made six figures and up a year. What was it about them that was so special?

They actually cared. They would go the extra mile giving you content, tutorials, step-by-step checklists, and more. They wanted to establish that they were an authority in their niche by teaching you. When you teach someone something, they will remember you long after the interaction. Especially if what you taught brings actual transformation to their life, big or small. They've built trust, and background information mattered less.

Show Passion for What You Do: Dr. Eric Thomas is a motivational speaker from Detroit who rose to stardom from a YouTube video. In the video, he's challenging a group of troubled youth about how dedicated they are to success. He is being aggressive, calling them out for their partying and lack of effort. His voice is loud and even straining at times. He cares, it's clear he gives a damn. That passion has led him to well over 50 million views, and that's a modest estimate.

Make Connections: In the 90's, many stores referred customers to a rival, if they didn't carry an item. It was great marketing, helping to build trust. You should do this when it comes to building relationships. If you know two individuals who should connect, make that introduction. When you help create a new opportunity for someone, that shows them you actually care.

Don't be Stingy with Your Network: Hoarding information and contacts is a hallmark characteristic of a taker. When two people match up well, and you refuse to make the connection because you think you get nothing out of it. I have made countless connections that turned into six-figure deals and even marriages. Those same people have come back and made life changing introductions for me in return. But I didn't expect a return either. I'll dig more into later.

Good stories

Research by Jeremy Hsu for Scientific American found that *"personal stories and gossip make up 65% of our conversations."* This is the reason TMZ, Media Takeout, and

National Enquirer are huge platforms. I'm not a fan of gossip, but I'm a fan of personal stories. Stories you use to teach, connect, and sell helps to create a great lasting impression.

Stories that teach. Martin Luther King Jr. became memorable because he preached in parables. Parables are small stories like Jesus told in the Bible. They serve as metaphors for a moral or spiritual lesson. Those are some of the earliest stories told that teach lessons.

Most of the early childhood cartoons we watched were stories laced with a lesson learned at the end. You can still borrow from those techniques to do the same as adults. One of my favorite books is *"The Richest Man in Babylon"* a fiction about money that follows a narrative.

When you use a story to teach, you connect with someone on a spiritual level. You sync up, the receiver connects with the storyteller emotionally and even biochemically. Have you ever told someone something and they retell you the same story later? They forgot you were the one that told them in the first place. Yes, that's what happens when you use narratives.

Stories that sell. Speaking with branding expert Marty Neumeier I learned that a brand is all about producing a gut feeling. That definition tells you everything that you need to know. If you can tell a story that shows people how to feel, you may just capture that sale. The best story is a story that your potential customer can see themselves in. Paint the picture.

Copywriting is also a great skill to learn to effectively tell a story. You don't have to be a master at this but, get the basics of a story that sells down. There is a formula most marketers use that dates back to the 1800's called AIDA:

A – Attention (Awareness): attract the attention of the customer.

I – Interest: raise customer interest by focusing on and demonstrating advantages and benefits (instead of focusing on features, as in traditional advertising).

D – Desire: convince customers that they want and desire the product or service and that it will satisfy their needs.

A – Action: lead customers towards taking action and/or purchasing.

You got jokes? Who doesn't love to laugh? Being someone with a great personality helps in making a great lasting impression. Laughter makes people happy, the most valuable feeling in the world.

Read, read, and read more!

The more you know, the more you increase your ability to hold interesting conversations. You can accomplish this by reading books ranging from history to psychology. I remember reading a blog from dating expert Tariq Nasheed. He emphasized every man should have what he called a "mouthpiece." In other words the gift of gab in order to attract women. That goes beyond dating, you need this skill if you want people to remember you in any situation.

Everyone you meet has a challenge they are dealing with.

Some people have small challenges, some people have large ones. The more you read, you are able to help solve their problem by recommending or using knowledge from a book.

Forget about it

This is the most important step of all when it comes to leaving a lasting impression. Too many people are looking for "credit" or some form of repayment rather than providing value to the people they want attention from. The best way to become magnetic is to go hard providing value to people, and then move on. Don't look for praise, recognition, or hook ups. Just do good.

The spiritual way of thinking about this is Karma. Karma simply means: do good things and get good things in return. You reap what you sow. Karma doesn't discriminate, it also works for bad things.

Another way to think of it is as a strategy. Bestselling author Ryan Holiday calls this the "Canvas Strategy." His advice is to *"Find and make canvases for other people to paint on."* Clear their path to victory. Instead of just making people look good, help them actually get better.

This chapter gave you all the tools. Give people great books to read. Connect them to people they will flourish with. Teach them new ways to deal with their challenges.

"The Roman's had a loose word for the concept: anteambulo and it meant a person who cleared the path in front of their patron.

If you can do that successfully, you secure a quick and educational power position."- Ryan Holiday

The after wow

Everything is by design. John Maeda, celebrated designer and technologist, taught me to design for the "after wow." What he meant by this was learning to design for the lasting impression and feeling people will have with your product. Life should be designed the same way. When you create relationships that give real value you create an effect that can last for a lifetime. Many call this a legacy.

The moment you embody this philosophy, your life will change, I promise. Remember to always leave a positive lasting impression.

WAKE UP RICH

"Stop trying to impress, start trying to improve" – Anthony
Frasier

Every day the alarm clock on my phone goes off at 5 am.
Waking up early is more than just a habit, it's necessary.
As an entrepreneur, I live a busy life. Once I get my day
started, it doesn't stop until I'm done working hours later.
When you're winding things down, you've already been
through a chunk of the thirty thousand thoughts humans
get per day.

That's negative thoughts, positive thoughts, and all other
emotions. These thoughts may be big, or barely
detectable. No matter how you feel, they are there, all
thirty thousand of them. The morning is your time to fill
your mind with the thoughts you need to succeed before
the day gets started. Otherwise, the day will just volunteer
them to you.

In addition to waking up early, the thoughts that perme-
ate my mind help to set the tone for the level of pro-

ductivity I can expect to anticipate for the day ahead. Thoughts become reality. Have you just known you were going to have a bad day and you actually did? Where your mind is when you wake up in the morning can have a negative or positive impact on the next twenty-four hours and your success as a whole.

Being a full-time entrepreneur means you own your schedule. To those who work traditional jobs, it can seem like this type of freedom means you get to lay around and watch tv all day. In reality, you could do this, but don't expect to see any progress in your goals if you make this choice. Hustle waits for no one. While you are still in bed, your competition is out there getting ahead.

When you wake up early and stay accountable for how you spend your time, you will become more productive. Spend that extra time in the morning to engage in activities that help you get better mentally, physically, emotionally, and spiritually.

Vishen Lakhiani, founder of *Mindvalley* has a perfect story on personal development. After starting Mindvalley in 2004, Vishen realized he was running a failing business. He felt overwhelmed, stressed, and depressed for four years straight. Everything he built started to collapse, nothing was working.

Then in 2008, something changed. He called it a shift. After one year of being in debt, the next year he became a millionaire. After one year of being miserable, the next year he became happy. What was that shift? It was a change in the way he thought. He went through what he describes as the four states of mind:

Negative Spiral – This is when everything is just not going right. You aren't happy with your life now, and you have no vision for the future.

Current Reality Trap – When you are content, but you still lack vision and enthusiasm for the future. Living day to day with no real goals on where you want to be will leave you feeling trapped like there is no way out of the cycle you are in.

Stress and Anxiety – When you have a vision for where you want to be in the future, but hate where you are at in life now.

State of Flow – When you are completely happy with life right now. But, you also have a vision of where you want to be in the future.

Vishen found a way to be happy now and excited about later. You can do the same by choosing to prepare for the struggles of everyday life while also being optimistic about the future. Having ups and downs is inevitable. But, the amount of time that you stay down instead of up is preventable. That's the difference maker.

So what does all of this have to do with the morning? When you wake up in the morning, you wash up and brush your teeth before going out. You wouldn't leave the house without washing your body, so why would you leave without washing your mind? That's when a morning routine comes in handy

The morning routine I developed is influenced by James Altucher's "daily practice." Every day do something that physically, mentally, spiritually, and emotionally helps you grow 1%. There are three hundred sixty-five days in the year. If you practice this routine you have the potential to grow by 365% by this same time next year. That's a complete turnaround.

The key to maintaining a routine is not to strive for perfection but overall consistency and mindfulness about the state of mind you plan to spend your day in. You will miss days, and some mornings just not have it in you. That's fine, just don't make a habit out of it.

Mental

The best mental exercise is writing down ten ideas a day. The purpose is to develop a creative muscle that will help you think quicker and better. You challenge yourself by choosing topics that will make you sweat. For example, "10 ideas to help Spotify make more money." At first, you will come up with some great obvious answers fast. When you start getting to number 8, it may take you longer.

Reading a few pages of a good book could also help you.

Physical

The obvious activity to accomplish this is exercise. You can buy something as small as a Kettlebell to help you exercise. There are also mobile apps that help you do exercises that take a few minutes without the need for gym equipment. If you have time to go to the gym, then you are good to go. You can also go for a run, or something as simple as taking a walk.

Physical can also mean getting a good amount of sleep the night before. The common theme you hear in the entrepreneur community is the bragging of no sleep, but a lack of sufficient sleep is quite dangerous. A lack of sleep hurts your hustle the same way drugs and alcohol can. Some days you will pull all-nighters, and your schedule will keep you up. But actively pursuing a position on team "no sleep" will be your demise.

Spiritual

I grew up in a Christian home. When I was young, my grandfather would tell me to get down on my knees and pray each morning. I'd thank God for my mother, my brother, my bed, my toys, etc. If you're religious, chances are you already have some kind of spiritual morning practice. But, what if you aren't religious?

This is where the heavy lifting gets done. I'm a big believer in meditation. Meditation allows you to mentally plan your day, show gratitude and visualize your future. All it takes is 20 minutes each morning. This isn't just spiritual, it's science.

When I tell people to meditate they usually get spooked out. People think meditation has to be done sitting down, legs crossed, chanting a phrase. Meditation could be as simple as laying in bed, putting on headphones, and playing an audio file. My suggestion is to browse YouTube for guided meditations and pick one or two you can do consistently.

Emotional

Emotional activities can be done throughout the day but start in the morning. Be around family you love. Stay with people and friends that give you energy. Nothing is worse than having someone snatch the positive energy from you. Negative situations can be your own fault if you don't separate from people like this.

You can also use this as an opportunity to create a journal. Write a few truths every morning. This can be a good way to transfer emotional thoughts out of your mind and onto paper. Let it live there instead. (see chapter Write Everything Down)

The Results

I discovered these practices about three years ago. Ever since then, my life has changed. I would not be writing these words you are reading right now if I didn't find a way to love myself and get my mind right in the morning. This truly helped me to focus my energy positively and not concern myself with the progress of others.

The thoughts I'm able to create in the morning fuel every decision I've made to get to this point. I have made mistakes, but my thoughts turned them into lessons. Because of this, I wake up rich every single day. The joy you will get from being happy now, is something money can't buy.

Good morning.

HOW TO FAIL

"The only difference between a winner and a loser is a winner plays until he wins" – Big KRIT

Statistics say about 50% of new businesses fail in their first five years and I've contributed to that number several times. Yet despite how "normal" it is to fail, I can't really recall a time when it didn't sting a little (or a lot) that an idea I had didn't work out the way I had hoped it would. There is nothing I can say that can change the way failure makes you feel. It hurts. My goal instead is to change the way you see failure. Perspective is your greatest friend when it comes to dealing with business pitfalls.

When people hear the word failure they think of the worst possible scenarios that failing can produce. You may fear the loss of your house, family, money, or in some cases your life. All of the things we fear losing are called risks. Not all risks are created equal. Some people have smalls risks to take while others have massive ones. However ultimately, if you aren't willing to take a risk, you just aren't willing to be successful.

When you decide to become an entrepreneur, at some point you will come face to face with a risk. It is in this moment, where you will learn the most about yourself. Are you willing to leave your job? Are you willing to go into debt? Are you willing to do all these things, even though you may still fail?

Risks are hard enough when taking them only affects us, but for some people, our risks can have implications on the ones we love as well. My mother wasn't an entrepreneur but she took a risk to move me and my brother to a better neighborhood. She put a lot on the line, and even had to get a second job at times. She was willing to lose out on having any kind of friends or activities so my brother and I could have a better life. Working from 7:00 in the morning until 10:00 in the evening, there was no guarantee we would turn out fine, but she took that risk anyway. Because of her willingness to take a risk on my behalf, you're reading these words.

Sometimes when we take a risk great things happen as in the example of my mother's risk for her children. Then, other times, we take a risk and lose things (whether permanent or temporary) that are very important to us. In those moments of loss, it is easy to feel like a failure. Yet that is not always the truth because experiencing an isolated failure is not the same.

What's the difference between failure and defeat? These words may seem similar but in my world of entrepreneurship, they are different. Failure means you lost the battle (and you will have many battles as an entrepreneur), defeat, on the other hand, means you lost the war. Often when you fail, you can get back up, defeat means you lost the ability to. Failure, unlike defeat, leaves the door open to try again. It may hurt a lot, but what doesn't kill you makes you stronger.

Failure makes you smarter. I learned at an early age to not touch a hot stove. But, only after getting burned a few times. That left me with two options. Either I'll go put some gloves on, or I'll find something better to do. That's entrepreneurship. Every failure presents an opportunity to learn. Find the lesson in the pain. What did you do wrong? What could have been better? Was it out of your control?

Once your perspective changes, each situation connects you to the next one. You understand that risk brings you closer to success, even though it make take a few tries. You understand that failure is just an opportunity to learn a better way. With a new perspective, you'll realize the door of success is often hidden behind the door of failure.

At times, it may seem like others get to that door of success quicker than you, but it's important to never compare your struggle to the progress of others. Rarely do we see their seeds being planted, just the flowers blooming. You don't know what that person has been through. You don't know the full story, just the one they decided to tell.

My favorite example of overcoming failure is the story of American inventor Thomas Edison. Thomas Edison's old lab is minutes away from me in New Jersey. As I toured his factory, I ended up staying longer in his library than anywhere else along the tour. I was hoping some of that genius could rub off on me.

He used the two-story library as his office, and it looks like it's never been touched since he left. What caught my eye is what I saw positioned in the corner of the room. A bed. What kind of man puts a bed in his library? Someone obsessed with learning from failure.

It's reported that Edison conducted over 1,000 experiments to get a working lightbulb. He did close to 10,000 experiments for the alkaline storage battery. Risk after risk. Failure after failure. Each time learning what he did wrong the previous attempt. His perspective on failure was his key to success.

For the average person, it wouldn't take 1,000 failures to walk away from an idea. In fact, many of us walk away after the first fail. But Edison is an example of perseverance and determination. If he tried 1,000 times and did not get discouraged then you can too. This is a man whose teachers claimed he was "too stupid" to learn anything. History shows us that he was far from stupid and maybe they just didn't know failure was a better teacher than they were.

In words of Thomas Edison himself: *"Our greatest weakness lies in giving up. The most certain way to succeed is always to try just one more time."* One of the best ways to recover from failure is to recognize and address what may have lead to it in the first place. Sometimes when we fail, we just focus on the end result and never pay much attention to the contributing factors which may have led to what ultimately happened, but taking a little time to examine the root problems can help us to avoid them on the next time around.

In my experience, there are four key types of failure that most entrepreneurs experience. I've outlined them below:

#1 Ourselves: Yep, that's right. It's easy to point your finger at others (employees, partners, spouses, etc.) such when things don't work out the way we'd like them to. But, in all honesty, that's often a counterproductive way of bouncing back. Because ultimately, you are responsible for your success, which means, you have to be in the hot seat before you ask anyone else to sit there. As a leader, you have to be willing to take the blame no matter what. Usually, we shy away from blame because we fear what people will think about us. You aren't learning from your situation if you're not prepared to take responsibility. What other people think is not more important than your personal growth.

#2 Outside forces: Sometimes there truly is some other force besides yourself that caused you to fail. For one of my startups, I had a huge partnership lined up. The partner company went bankrupt shortly after our agreement. There are other cases like natural disasters. Hurricane Sandy wiped out many businesses in New York and New Jersey. Though it wasn't their fault, they wouldn't be able to rebuild if they didn't take action. Those business owners decided to not complain, and change their perspective.

#3 Bad Planning: A famous business saying states *"if you fail to plan, you plan to fail,"* and this is very true. While I'm not a fan of traditional business plans, you do need some kind of plan and strategy for your business. It doesn't matter how big or small you think you are, lay out a plan. Create a set of three goals you want to reach every three months, and start hammering away. If you don't have a plan, you don't have direction and there's chance your business will fail shortly after getting off the ground.

#4 Bad Idea: It may sting to hear, but some business ideas are just...bad. There are two reasons a bad idea can cause you to fail. The first is you haven't picked a good market. A good idea connects to people beyond the surface level. You might have picked a niche that was too broad or way too small. You may have also picked a niche that doesn't match your product. You can't sell expensive items to an audience that can't afford it. On the flip side, there are some markets that don't like cheap products. Find your balance.

The second reason is, you are too in love with your idea. Yes, you need some level of passion for what you are building. But, you also have to be willing to make adjustments when needed. Learn how to take advice and constructive criticism. The more you do research, you may start to see your idea fall apart. This is not a bad thing. Put yourself out of business before your competition does. Keep improving. Don't fail when you don't have to.

Preventing failure

#1 Experiment: I'm a big fan of *The Lean Startup* method. It encourages entrepreneurs to create a product with the smallest features. Once built, you can measure and learn from the people using it. Use what you learn to add, subtract, or pivot all together to something different. This method of "build, measure, learn" is used in the tech industry. But, this way of thinking can be applied to any business. It allows you to fail fast and early.

#2 Do your homework: Research as much as you can. My brother used to tell me, "you pay for what you don't know." Not just with money, you pay with time and energy. I talk about the importance of reading in this book many times. It's essential to your growth as an entrepreneur.

#3: Find a mentor: Getting advice and guidance from an experienced entrepreneur is priceless. My suggestion is to seek mentors in several areas of your life. Focusing just on business can leave you unbalanced.

Tim Ferris, author of *"The 4-Hour Work Week"* gets mentorship requests all the time. But he says entrepreneurs are going about it all wrong. *"Asking someone to be a mentor is a way for them never to be a mentor,"* he says. When you approach someone, it's important that you don't sound like you are giving them a job. The best approach is asking if you can send them a question every once in awhile via email. Over time, you will see your relationship with that person grow. This isn't the case for every potential mentor.

Another communication flaw most people have is not knowing how to listen. Sometimes I watch Shark Tank and it kills me to see a stubborn entrepreneur who denies good feedback. Your potential mentor will feel like she is wasting her time with you if you refuse to listen to her advice. Learn how to ask the right questions and listen. These steps are critical in the beginning of a mentor/mentee relationship.

#4 Be the dumbest person in the room. Surround yourself with people smarter than you. A bad team does not just mean you have bad people around you. A bad team means you don't have people around you to fill in the gaps. Every person on your squad should be more talented or smarter than you in a certain area. Fill in those gaps. It was Henry Ford who said, *"I am not the smartest, but I surround myself with competent people."* Another titan David Ogilvy tells us, *"If you ever find a man who is better than you are – hire him. If necessary, pay him more than you would pay yourself."*

Failure is a mental exercise. The more you go to the gym, the stronger you get. The key is to not get defeated.

THE HATER OUTSIDE YOUR HEAD

"Criticism is something we can avoid easily by saying nothing, doing nothing, and being nothing." – Aristotle

In 2009, I met Gerard Williams. Gerard became popular online under the alias *"Hip Hop Gamer."* People flocked to his video game reviews because of his Brooklyn accent and live energy. He stood out. At that time, it was rare to see a black face in the gaming industry, but he was making his mark.

Gerard gave me my first real look at how gaming worked behind the scenes. I was a fish out of water with my first website, so he showed me the ropes. He would fly me to press events with him and it was amazing to me to see how so many well-known figures in the video game world knew who he was.

Being this close to someone who was so well-known had a profoundly positive impact on me, but there was a dark side to the popularity. I have been an entrepreneur for almost 10 years now, and nothing has matched the amount of hate I saw one man get. I've had my fair share of "haters." but nothing like the mix of racism, jealousy, envy, and people who criticised him for being stereotypical.

It was sad to see so many people campaign against ending his career. They wanted him gone, and the unfortunate reality is that they will want you gone too if you reach a certain level of success...be prepared for it.

Why Haters Hate

One of the top reasons people hate on others has nothing to do with us and everything to do with them. Many people are frustrated about where they are in their life and compare themselves to you. They don't know your story, struggle, or sacrifices. They just see the good, and they don't understand why you have it. They feel you don't deserve it and they are jealous.

You may even experience hate from friends and family. They don't want you to progress because they don't want to become irrelevant. I had a girlfriend tell me hurtful things despite me progressing in my career because she feared she wouldn't get as much attention as I became more successful.

Hate can also be taught. Most children learn to be prejudice towards another race from their parents and communities. The lack of diversity in any field also plays a role. If people grow up only seeing a one race in the media, they may get a little uncomfortable when change happens and they may even invest time and energy in getting rid of people in positions that that don't look like them. When you are doing something amazing, hate is inevitable. When you are being disruptive and changing the status quo, people will get angry with you.

But not everything negative we hear about ourselves from others is "hate." People have a right to legitimately dislike our work challenge us and dislike what we are about without it automatically being a symptom of jealousy or racism. Among millennials, "hater" is being thrown around so loosely that legitimate feedback gets ignored.

"Your most unhappy customers are your greatest source of learning." – Bill Gates

Hate vs criticism

Criticism can be a valuable tool in the life of an entrepreneur because it can make us aware of our areas of growth. However, criticism doesn't always feel good. We usually don't like to hear that something we've produced isn't as good as we think it is. For this reason, it is easy to confuse valuable criticism with hate and see them as the same thing. The reason so many people throw criticism and hate in the same bucket is because they fear it. Criticism should be embraced, and hate should be ignored.

Below are a few statements that come from haters and a few that come from constructive critics. Can you tell which is which?

"That red hat looks stupid on you"

"Red doesn't fit you, the green goes better with your jacket"

"I don't like the where the home button is placed on the app. Nobody has hands like that. Did a blind person make this app?"

"This app is garbage, save your money"

Some of the statements are meant to make you feel bad, and some are meant to help you make you aware of ways you can improve. Not all legit criticism comes off in a nice way and may even come from a person who genuinely dislikes you. But, if it is grounded in logic and can help you improve your business, extract the valuable part and ignore the rest. That's the difference on the most basic level.

So why does it mess with our head? Negativity sticks. We become fixated on the bad parts, and never hear the advice part. For example, if you write an article and see positive reviews, the one bad review is likely going to be on your mind all day long. Once that happens it will start to lower your self-confidence if you are not careful because you may be tempted to weigh the value of your work on that one solitary comment despite the abundance of affirming statements that were shared. The best way to prepare for this is to come to terms with the fact that there will always (ALWAYS) be people who simply do not like what you create. Having this expectation will lessen the blow of actually seeing and hearing comments because you've mentally prepared yourself for what is simply one of the biggest realities of being an entrepreneur: haters are gonna hate.

Snakes

There are different levels of haters. Some of them are very comfortable with letting you know, up front, that they don't like you or your work. That's often the easiest kind of hater to deal with because their dislike for you is very obvious and so you know what to expect from them. On the other hand, there is another kind of hater who is harder to spot because they aren't as outward with regard to how they feel about you. Often these are people who are close to you. You may have no idea but deep down they have ill feelings towards you. I call them snakes.

Snakes are known for their sneaky manner of attacking, often going unnoticed by their ability to blend in well with their surroundings. In plain terms, snakes in your life may look very much like the people you've carefully chosen to be around you because you trust them. Snakes are more dangerous than a normal hater because they can do more harm to you because you are often more vulnerable to them.

How do you spot a snake? If you're lucky you can start to pick up vibes and small things like facial expressions and also their reactions to your success. When people are genuinely down for you, they will be genuinely happy for you when you reach a milestone or are recognized for an accomplishment. However, snakes will often downplay your milestones or they will subtly discourage you from going after what you want under the guise of being concerned or looking out for you. Picking up on these subtle things can help you see a snake disguised as a friend. So the moment you get a sense that something is wrong, you should call it out. Don't let something small build up over time, it's best to get to the bottom of it fast.

Other times, though, snakes are a lot tougher to spot, and the harsh reality is, you may just get bitten by one. In this case, karma is key. When a snake reveals themselves you may be tempted to retaliate, expose them or gossip. But stay cool, take time to heal from your snake bite and let life handle the rest.

Handling haters

My first website was hacked by a former business partner, it was a low blow and could have laid the foundations of an ugly war. However, rather than retaliate, I told my team we were going to start a new site, and to not engage with the people who stole our previous one. Why? Because the old partner wanted to cause a stir, but he could only do that if the lines of communication were open. Instead, I chose to cut him off. When you play with fire you get burned and there would have definitely been flames if I would have reacted in the way he wanted me to. Sometimes it's not that easy when major damage is done by a hater, but If it doesn't affect you financially or physically then what reason do you have to engage?

When haters get out of hand, they are likely acting out of a deep-seated jealousy or insecurity. To counteract this, keep in mind that you must be doing something right if someone wants to use their precious energy and time on you. Be flattered but keep it moving.

Remember my friend Gerard? I asked him one day how he dealt with his haters. He told me he prays for them. Gerard was a dedicated Christian and wasn't shy about it. I took his advice. Anytime I would come across a hater online or in person, I'd wish them the best and separate myself. Do the same and truly mean it, because success heals all wounds.

CORE VALUES

"I'm a person that's grounded in faith and believe that my core values, motivation, inspiration, draw from a conception of the world in that way." – Cory Booker

The quest for perfectionism is a recipe for failure. For years, I struggled with depression, anxiety, self-doubt, and heartbreak trying to be perfect for people. I tried to live life to other people's standards while completely ignoring what was perfect for me. I was miserable.

On it's deepest level, my focus on meeting the unrealistic standards of others was rooted in the fact that I hadn't defined my own my purpose in life. I had goals, but my goals weren't strong enough. My goals were based on material things and not purpose. Purpose is bigger than material possessions. Having a purpose means having goals that will leave a legacy, something that will live forever long after you are off this earth. Having purpose means you have a foundation.

I often compare life to a house. When you begin to build

a house, usually the ground below it is uneven, shifty, and soft. To keep a house stable, you have to build it on top of a solid foundation. Foundation is concrete, strong and can't be moved. It keeps the house together. It bears the load of the structure on top and serves as an anchor against natural forces.

Much like a house, our own lives must be rooted in a firm foundation. Having a purpose driven foundation requires rules much like a code of conduct. This foundation serves as a reminder to us of what we value as we go day by day making decisions for our business and life.

These rules will give you self-worth, self-confidence, and purpose. When you know what you stand for, then you live your life to the standards that you set for yourself. Perfection is following your own value system to the best of your ability.

When you create a set of core values for yourself you start to build your own philosophy. Marcus Aurelias was one of the most popular stoic philosophers. His best work is a book called "Meditations." Meditations were personal writings and private notes about himself. He kept rules in here reminding himself how to act and behave.

His meditations were never intended to be made public, yet the work was so great it created a wave of people embodying the same philosophies. Some becoming stoics themselves. He created core values for himself and changed lives thousands of years later as a result. I believe you can do the same.

How to create your core values

Like Marcus Aurelius, before creating a set of values to go by you have to be bold. That means saying no to opportunities that look good on paper, but look bad on where you want your life to go. In this way, whenever you feel like you're being tempted to do something you aren't sure is a good idea or in line with your values, you will have them in writing to refer to.

To get started, take a notebook and begin to write these things down (see chapter Write Everything Down):

- Everything you care about
- How you want to be remembered when you're gone
- Things you don't want to do to make money
- How your spiritual beliefs help you every day
- The best qualities of people you look up to
- The worst qualities of people you don't like
- How you'd love to do business
- What a perfect day would look like to you in 5 years.
- How you think the world should work
- The biggest lessons you learned in life
- What makes you happy
- What makes you angry

Write as much as you can in one sitting. It may take you a few days coming back and forth to it, but be thoughtful in your words as you write.

When you have written as much as you can on all these subjects, you will discover new things about yourself. It may seem all over the place, but that's on purpose. Pick the biggest lessons from these writings and formulate a rule or statement from them. For example, I don't like people who lie to get ahead. So, I may have a core value that states "never lie to get ahead." There is no standard to how many values you can have. These writings will become a resource guide to what your core values can be.

When I made my core values, my life changed. I no longer had a fear of missing out. I made better decisions. I gained more respect. I became less thirsty. I slept good at night, despite walking away from deals that paid good, but I didn't like. I ended relationships with people who didn't make my life better. I'm a more perfect me because I understand what I stand for.

Having a foundation and core values is very important, but it doesn't guarantee that bad things won't come your way in life but it does give you a place to come back to if you need to refocus. Much like a home that has been destroyed in a storm, a firm foundation provides a capable cornerstone from which to rebuild. Yet without one, the house may be a lost cause or take more effort and resources to re-establish.

As an entrepreneur, you will need a strong set of values to guide you both personally and in business. When you have a set of core values for your company, you know what new products to create. You know what new features you want. You know what partnerships to form. Most of all, you know what to say no to. Before you ever start, it is absolutely essential that you decide what kind of person you will be and hold yourself accountable for having the integrity to always be true to who you are, no matter what.

MY STORY - PART TWO

Continued...

When I opened the letter I had written at the beginning of my high school career, I began to cry. I felt like I betrayed myself as I read the words filled with hope and promise that I had failed to fulfill. The letter charted a path for me to do well in school so that I could go to a good college. The letter also told me to learn how to use "computers" and use that to help my family. I didn't do any of those things. At that moment, I promised myself that all of my next steps would be centered on trying hard as I could to honor the contents of the letter even though high school was over.

Afterward, I went to a county college for about a year. I couldn't stand it there so I dropped out. I came to the conclusion school wasn't for me. If I was going to become successful I had to learn on my own style and pace. I learned about online journalism and started a video game review site with a group of friends. We got attention early on because we were one of the only websites that had a focus on black gamers.

Our website became so popular, we received special

attention from the game industry. This was the first real taste of success I had. While things were going well on the surface, my life was turning to shit underneath. Despite the success of the website, I had no money, my grandfather died, and on top of that, I was diagnosed with life-threatening high blood pressure. I didn't understand why this was happening to me.

To pay bills, I got a job at a retailer on their receiving dock. It was an overnight job. My task was to unload boxes from the trailer and help stock them in the store. So my days became long. Working on my website all during the day, then working on the truck all through the night. I wasn't sleeping, and my health got worse.

The managers treated me horribly. They'd insult me, tell me to do things that weren't my job, and they found it amusing. I needed the job, so I had to hold my tongue anytime I felt the need to retaliate. One day all my emotions just came to a head. When no one came to work, and I was left to unload an entire full truck by myself. I went to the back of the warehouse and just sat on the floor thinking "I can't live like this."

By the end of that day, I went to the manager and told him I would not be back next week. His reply was "yeah right, you'll be back." That was the last time I ever saw him.

After I quit my job, I went to the local library every day so I wouldn't be in the house all day. I hated being there when my mother came home because it made me feel like I failed her. While in the library I would read magazines and articles about successful tech startups. I was very interested in becoming involved in tech, so I searched until I found an ad for an internship at a tech startup.

A company in Montclair, NJ was hiring for college interns. I didn't have a college degree, but I had experience building a website from scratch, and I thought "what could someone who has been in a classroom for four years know that I don't? I've been in the trenches for the same amount of time. I saw that my website traffic was also better than theirs, so I figured I could use that as leverage.

I got a call in to interview for the internship. They hired me on the spot, and a month later I got bumped up to doing business development for a tech startup full time. I had set a goal and achieved it for the first time in my life. I took this time to learn as much as I could about building a startup from the founder Todd Hamilton. He took me under his wing and mentored me through the entire process.

Around this time, I also began to take better care of my health and weight. I bought a kettlebell and put myself on a strict diet. I was 340 pounds and brought my weight down to 250 pounds. I started to wing myself off high blood pressure medication, and I felt the best I had ever felt in my life.

Using what I learned from Todd, I sketched out the concept for a new app. Unfortunately, Todd's startup went under. I saw an opportunity to pitch my idea to the main investor and he loved it. I got an investment and a development team ready to build out my vision.

I saw an influential black social media figure Wayne Sutton tweet about a program. He was teaming up with another entrepreneur Angela Benton to create an accelerator for black tech startups. It was the first of it's kind. I'd get the opportunity to live in Silicon Valley, and learn from the people in the magazines I was reading. It was the last day to apply, so I rushed through the application. I didn't expect anything to happen, I kept focused on building my app.

The next week Angela called me to be part of the program. She informed me that CNN Black In America would be filming and they would begin as early as the following week. I was excited and nervous at the same time thinking: What if I get exposed? What if they realize I'm just some kid from Newark with no experience? I went through with it anyway.

I flew to Silicon Valley and pitched my company to Google executives the same day. I didn't care about my lack of formal education anymore. I decided to live in the moment, and take advantage of the opportunity.

While the other entrepreneurs were pitching, I snuck away and toured the Google campus. I found a spot where I could sit down and reflect. I thought about my life and asked myself the same question I asked when I was struggling: Why is this happening to me? Ironically it was the one- year anniversary of the day I left my job.

I figured out that the good and the bad were equal in my life. It was all about the reaction that made all the difference. Here are some takeaways I learned from my story up to that point that I hope can help you:

#1 Everything Happens for a Reason: It's cliche but that doesn't make it any less true. If I didn't struggle, I wouldn't have built up the mental stability for entrepreneurship. I feel like my life's experiences were the best preparation I could ever ask for.

#2 Hustle While you Wait: When things got rough, I still kept grinding. I knew deep down inside it was all going to pay off someday. Nothing worth having comes easy.

#3 Take Care of Yourself Before You Try to Take Care of Others: I desperately wanted to be successful, but my health put me on the sideline many times in my life. The best thing you can do for yourself and your family is to remain healthy.

#4 Do What Works for You Even if It's Unconventional: I wasn't a dummy. I couldn't focus or do well in school, but I knew I was smart. You have to figure out the best way to consume and comprehend information. The teacher and chalkboard style just wasn't cutting it for me.

#5 Make a decision and Live with It: We can't rewind time. There are some things I wish I could have done better. When you make a decision and things don't go the way you imagined, learn how to adapt. You can turn shit to sugar if you have a well thought out plan.

Thank you.

Special thanks to these individuals who directly and indirectly played a part in me writing this book.

Jimi Olaghere \ Gary Swaby

Soledad O'Brien \ Wanda Reynolds

Ted Peterson \ Mack Bonthera

Mujib A. Lateef \ James Altucher

Chris Guillebeau \ Angela Benton

My Grandmother Mamie Frasier

My Grandfather William Frasier. RIP.

The Phat Startup team, our community + friends!

I love you!

ABOUT THE AUTHOR

Anthony Frasier is best known for being one of the savvy founders of The Phat Startup, an integrated media company that produced resources for aspiring entrepreneurs. By leveraging Lean Startup methodology and drawing on the connections between entrepreneurship and hip hop, you can credit Frasier and his team for successfully creating the critically acclaimed Tech808 conference that highlighted some of the best minds in the tech industry.

His work has been featured on hit media outlets and documentaries such as Black Enterprise, Black Entertainment Television (BET), Black In America (CNN), CNN Money, USA Today, and Fast Company. He has been invited to speak for leading organizations, which include Lean Startup Conference, The Congressional Black Caucus, TED, SXSW, and many more. He was also named an innovator by AT&T, which highlighted black entrepreneurship to millions in TV spots aired nationally.

A serial entrepreneur, Frasier was the creator of a mobile startup called Playd and established an award-winning gaming site called The Koalition. As a freelance consultant, he advises, consults and coaches startups and small businesses on their product visions, business development efforts and social and digital media initiatives to propel their endeavors forward.

Outside of his work in the startup and entrepreneurial scene, you can find him actively involved in promoting a positive community impact for aspiring entrepreneurs in Newark, New Jersey as the creator of Brick City Tech. His philanthropic initiatives have been recognized by the Business Outreach Center, where he was granted the Award for Entrepreneurship and Community Impact.

I've had the pleasure to speak about tech entrepreneurship, economic empowerment, and personal development from the top Silicon Valley stages to classrooms in the heart of Newark, NJ. I love to take complex topics and make them simple and entertaining to learn about. Contact us to learn more!

speaking@AnthonyFrasier.com